Private Driver

True bl-

Confessions, Part 3

By

Harvey Jenkins MD PhD

Introduction

This book almost remained unwritten. Sometimes in the course of things, life steps in and redirects your path. That is what happened with this book. In the time since the last one in the Private Driver series, I have grown in ways that I could not imagine. Suffice it to say that a cage cannot contain a creative mind, whether you place yourself in that cage or someone else does.

I dedicate this book to **Harvette**, my sweet sister, biggest fan, and savior throughout life. She is my 'True Blue'. I will never be able to repay her for the guidance and support that only a big sister can give. To her, I promise to live up to my potential.

As you may have guessed, this book follows in the same vein of the previous ones in the "Private Driver" series, in that it pays homage to another iconic music album: *"True Blue"*. It was released in 1986, back when I was young and idealistic. Madonna's first two albums focused on making you dance. It was all about the groove. In this album, she abandoned the the Minnie Mouse vocals that made her famous and traded them for a consistently lower register, as well as a more introspective and mature message. It topped the charts in almost 30 countries and was the best-selling album by a female artist in the eighties. Its stunning video imagery, including the video for the song "Open Your Heart", where she portrays an exotic dancer in a cinematic peep show, contains a still frame, which is a re-creation of the True Blue Album cover, shot and edited by Herb Ritts. The video, like many from this album, tells a story more complex than the lyrics of song.

During my last several hundred miles on the road, the multiple references to "True Blue" became clear, making the title of this work and the story-telling within it happen easily and naturally. Life truly does mimic art, and vice versa.

Table of Contents

Chapter 1

Feel the Burn

The tough part of Uber is when you pick up someone who is really hurting inside. Drunk or not, they expect you to be their counselor. This is hard to do for someone whom you just met and barely know. In any event, they need you to say the right thing and may be show them the bright side of things and help make a bad situation better.

 Tonight was one of those tough times when I couldn't think of anything good to say. So, I did the best I could, though, because I knew she was counting on me.

I said "the good thing about *Herpes* is that you can only get it once.....and that burning sensation? It only happens once in a while....not all the time....and maybe during sex...so I'm told."

I'm not sure if it helped her that much. But the way her face scrunched up, I knew that it had affected her in a good way.

When she got out of the car, I realized that I would make a really bad bartender.

<White Heat>

Chapter 2

Bricktown

As we were driving down Shields Ave in downtown Oklahoma City, the rider, a businessman who was from out-of-town and who I had picked up from the Will Rogers Airport, noticed the entry to Bricktown.

"Bricktown. Hmmm. What is that?" he asked.

I said "it's our main downtown tourist area. There are lots of good clubs and restaurants there. Toby Keith and Kevin Durant's restaurants are there. You should really check it out while you are in town."

He said "Wow, it looks neat! But why do they call it "Bricktown". Is it kinda one of those older industrial areas that they re-vamped, with a lot of Brick buildings, maybe?"

I said "Nahh. I think they call it 'Bricktown', because late night, when the bars are about to close, you are liable to come outta there with a 'Brick' to the head."

I am really glad he didn't ask me about that restaurant in Bricktown called "Crabtown". It's name is so much harder to explain."

<Live To Tell>

Chapter 3

Church Porn

The day after Christmas, I picked up this pretentious' group of "twenty-something" *people* from the northside and took them to the Rockford Lounge on 23rd street. When we turned onto 23rd, we passed this church, and one of the passengers in the back said "See that church? I used to do their "IT" and their computers are *DIRTY*."

One of the girls in the group said "DIRTY? You mean that it had a lot of dust on it?

He said "No, I mean 'Dirty' as in 'Full of PORN'..."

As they gasped in horror, I took a long sigh, clenched the steering wheel tightly, kept my right eye on the road, as my left eye rolled in the back of my head out of annoyance. I felt like my brain had shut itself down for a critical update, like my iPhone, to prepare itself for the rest of the stupidity, I was gonna experience this night.

I said "M'kay. So, y'all are just finding out right now that people in the religious profession like porn? I got another obvious newsflash that you may not be aware of: Have y'all heard of Santa Claus? Well, he ain't real, either.

<Silence>

"And for that matter, maybe the porn you found on their computer was actually research they were doing for a sermon on 'Pornz' that week? Don't judge before you got all the facts."

<BAM>

"And, as far as that goes, the fact that you knew it was porn means you obviously have some experience and prior knowledge of the subject in the first place. So don't act like you were all shocked and disgusted by something you are already fully aware of.

<BAM>

"And lastly, the Lord don't like snitches. Think about that one while you are getting 'slizzard' at that bar you are getting ready to go to... exactly one day after the Lord's Birthday."

After a few moments of silence, like the kind you experience after a gun battle, the porn whisperer, said to me "Harvey, maybe you just need to focus on driving, bro."

And I said back to him "Put some damn RESPEK on my name, when you're asking me to do something."

I didn't get a tip when I dropped them off, but I felt so much better that I defended the privacy breach of that church.

<Papa Don't Preach>

Chapter 4

Greybushes

I picked up a group of middle-aged folks this evening and was driving them to Bricktown. One of them asked me to change the radio-station from "Watercolors" (Smooth jazz) to "The Heat" (a Hip-Hop station). I have an open mind towards people, but this choice did not make sense to me.

I said " Hmmm. M'kay, but y'all don't look like the average 'Hip-Hop' types."

One the guys clapped back "We may be 'Greybushes', but we still got 'game'."

<silence>

I just stared at him for a record amount of time without blinking or saying one word after he said that. My neck was too stiff to shake my head disapprovingly at that statement. "Greybushes", I thought, better be the name of the neighborhood that they live in or otherwise I'm gonna be sick.

It's sick 'muvas' like that that will always guarantee that there will be another book.

Also, I decided we clearly don't have enough churches in OKC if you got folks like this around, saying stuff like this...

<Open Your Heart>

Chapter 5

Irony

Thursday nights are not the usual party nights. It's even less likely a time to go out when it's 20 degrees outside with a windchill that makes it feel like you're driving in the Alaskan Yukon rather than Yukon, Oklahoma. Even still, I drove to Yukon about 15 miles west of Oklahoma City to pick up a rider. The rider I was to pick up texted to let me know exactly which apartment building in the complex she lived in, which is unusual. It is also helpful. It let me know that she was not going to be a "No Show" when I arrived and that she meant business. When she jumped in the car, she indicated that her destination was "Graham's", a country-themed disco and watering hole, known for its magnetic effect on people with Cowboy hats, tight jeans and boots, who like to two-step to songs by Miley Cyrus' dad. It is also on the outskirts of the downtown Oklahoma City area.

As we drove toward OKC, she indicated we had to stop along the way to pick up a friend. Instead of giving me a specific address, she said she would simply direct me to his place. In the time we drove before picking up her friend, she revealed some biography. She mentioned that she was a college student and she liked using Uber. She even used to use it twice a week to get to college in Norman, Oklahoma, a distance of 25 miles each way. She said that it was really inconvenient and expensive, but she did not have any other options, since she did not have her license back then. I admired the spirit of this young "working girl" finding time to pursue higher-education, even without a car. It sounded like "partying" and"letting loose" on a Thursday night was probably a moment that she had spent the entire week earning through studying and working. She also mentioned that because she planned on drinking, she was using Uber. It was the smart thing to do. Young people, I began thinking, are becoming so smart and socially aware, unlike the previous generation.

 As we are driving, her knowledge of her friend's place seemed to be a bit dubious, as we made so many sudden turns and even had to backtrack at one point.   Meanwhile, she texted her friend, who seemed a bit impatient, to let him know that we would be there soon. We approached a cul-de-sac, and she said " Oh wait, I think that's his house."

It was indeed his house and he came to the car. I was suspicious, however, that this may have been a blind-date or some awkward Craigslist Casual Encounter to which I was getting ready to be an unwilling witness. Brian, a husky, twenty-something combination hipster with a little Duck Dynasty mixed in, jumped in the car, next to Lisa, and greeted her. He remarked at how much he liked my car, and that he should consider driving for Uber, possibly not realizing that the car belonged to me and not Uber.   With that, we headed to Graham's.

The conversation for the twelve-mile duration was strange.   Brian talked about how he couldn't wait to down the first three beers.   Lisa concurred and indicated how she couldn't wait to do some shots.   It was becoming clearer from the conversation, that this wasn't a date. They were more like classmates.

She confirmed their relationship to each other and how they knew each other when she said "Umm, It's kinda weird that we are actually celebrating getting our licenses back by going out and getting drunk."

Brian countered " Yea, I guess   But mine wasn't a *real* DUI. I just blew a 1.0.   Same thing for those two other DUI's I got."

Since I thought it would be rude to say "WT-Actual-F?", my eyes rolled in my head in disbelief that I just drove a couple to Graham's to celebrate an important occasion -- both of them getting their licenses back after a DUI.

Now, I've seen everything.

<Where's The Party?>

Chapter 6

A Girl Can Never be too Careful

It is clear. Some people will never be comfortable with getting into a stranger's car. Let's face it. Our parents have all raised us this way. Uber and Lyft undoubtedly have considered this cultural obstacle when they started these companies. They have calculated that saving a lot of money will always trump the lessons your mama tried to teach you. For most riders, the calculation was correct. For others, not so much.

I picked up a rider named Maddie from a northside Oklahoma City neighborhood. After waiting about four minutes in front of her house, she emerged with a large bag. Rather than getting into the car as most riders do, she hunched down and peered into the closed rider-side window at me. With stealthy eyes, she looked towards the back of the car, and then back at me. I signaled to her to get into the car with hand motions and using my most welcoming and disarming smile that I could muster. With a little hesitation, she slowly got in and began fidgeting with the massive purse she brought with her. I assumed she must be really new to ride-sharing.

She pulled out a large metal ring, the size of a large notebook binder rings or Jody Watley earrings which contained a web of charms. Unlike a charm bracelet, the charms dangling from this metal ring were different. In addition to containing keys dangling from the metal ring, what looked like a lipstick container was present as were also some pendulous self-defense charms. I could make out what looked like a tiny Swiss-army knife and a mini-can of mace. She seemed to jangle the ring like a warrior, with what she thought was a major can of whoop-ass. I was quite confused by her display. This was not a strange, beautiful island she was getting onto. Nor was it an episode of survivor.

"Is that Mace on that thing?" I asked.

She looked me directly in the eye as if simultaneously informing me and warning me, "Yes, it's MACE. And I'm not afraid to use it. A girl can never be too safe these days."

After a few seconds of our eyes locking, verifying that I understood exactly the meaning of what she was saying, I opened up my center console glove box, between the seats, and pulled out my taser. When I closed the console, I placed it on top and gave it a couple of pats.

I said "Girl, I know exactly what you mean. This is 'Tazee Mae', my taser."

<Silence>

"Thankfully, I've only had to use her twice. You remember that song by Adele *Set fire to the Rain?*" Well, you shoulda seen that last drunk girl I had to use it on. It didn't 'set fire to the rain', but it certainly lit up her retinas like a 40 ft drive-in movie screen. I swear I could see scenes from every movie she had seen since the third-grade on the projection glow on her retinas, plus practically every one she talked to that day."

<Silence>

I said "Mmm-humm....Yup!"

Quite abruptly, she opened the back door and hopped out, only saying she forgot that she was supposed to stay home that night. I drove away. I guess what a lot of 'crazy folks' don't know is that I can pretend to be even crazier than they are.

That is not a game they can win with me.

If this was a game of real-life "Survivor". I wanted to make sure I was the winner and got off the island on my own terms. I doubt she will ever use ride-share again. But that's okay.

<La Isla Bonita>

Chapter 7

For the Love of Waffles

Driving for a ride-share company can be murder on your car. Most people who sign up to drive don;t realize the expense they will incur on car maintenance and repairs due to the excessive mileage you log. Having driven enough to qualify for any NASCAR-sanctioned event, I know what I am talking about, and I've seen my share of breakdowns and malfunctions. Over time, I've learned what things I can ignore for awhile, and what things need addressed immediately. The 'engine light' warning coming on is one of those things. It is also the most recent reason I had to take the Escalade in for an immediate check-up. Unfortunately, this episode required I leave my car at the shop while they figured out not only what the problem was, but how to maximize whatever the charge would be. I know my dealer too well. Three days later, I got the call from the dealer letting me know that the problem had been fixed. I prayed it was something simple, like a faulty sensor, but no such luck. The damage turned out to be a $2,000 repair, which effectively wiped out my profit-margin for a couple of months. Thankfully, they had given me a loaner vehicle, which is good, but I couldn't use a loaner car to drive for Uber is prohibited.

When I got to the dealer to return the loaner car, pay the bill, and pick up my repaired vehicle, the service tech called for the assistant to bring up my car.
The assistant asked which one. He winked condescendingly and said "The one with the eyelashes, Pfft!!!"

I like my carlashes. The silver eyelash adornments above and under the headlights makes my car less intimidating and menacing. Let's face it. Black escalades carry with them an associations with gang activity and the "Thug Life". The eyelashes soften this stereotype. And before a rider can become afraid of it or make judgments about me, they are usually to busy laughing or smiling at how cute my car is.   Similarly, the cops at 2AM think the driver of my vehicle is probably a cute, blonde sorority girl, rather than a big old burly black man.   Because of this, I think adding the carlashes has saved me from more than a few stops by the cops.

From the service tech's tone, I thought to myself "how friggin' rude!" And since I'd been in the mood for confrontations for weeks, I said " Oh Wait, Do 'WE' have a problem with cars with "eyelashes", Mister Macho Manly, Str8 boy?"

He looked shocked and surprised that I called him out, but he didn't say a word.

I said "Well, keep playing 'that game' and my shoe may end up putting a 'waffle print' on the left-side of your head, and the only place you'll be able to work with that "look" is the circus"

<silence>

He said "Did you say "Waffle"?

I wasn't expecting him to come back at with that, But I said "yes, 'Waffle'", with a little hesitation in my voice.

He goes, "O-M-G , I LOOOOOVEEE Waffles!!" with the excitement of a young sorority girl during rush week.

<silence>

He continues,"With blueberries and maple syrup!!!"

<Then the sorority rush fever started coming over me>.

We looked at each other awkwardly over our mutual love of waffles. We didn't know whether to hug each other, kiss each other or just shake hands. I chose shaking hands. Since, I don't kiss any strangers any more since that Ebola scare last year.

I just said "Absolutely. You can come over to my place later if you want. My waffles aren't as good as IHOP's, but with enough whip cream you can't even tell... and they're Gluten-free!!!"

When I was driving away I thought it was so cool how a volatile situation which could have been horrible got turned into something really cool. Remember y'all, despite our misunderstandings and differences, deep down we all have things in common. It's part of being human.

<Love Makes the World Go Round>

Chapter 8

Jaime Jaime

The week following May graduation is generally a "dead" week for Uber and Lyft Drivers. The student's going home turn the university town into a ghost town. I really don't know why I ventured to drive during that week, other than the fact that you can always find something good when you scrape the bottom of any barrel.

I hit ghost-town 'paydirt' when I got the call to pick up a rider from the New York Pizza shop in Campus Corner, the central party hub of the University of Oklahoma. I should have known anyone who remained in town would most likely be found there. The fact that the OKC Thunder, our NBA basketball team was playing in the Western Conference Championship Finals was the "full moon" that drew the ghosts, ghouls and vampires still left in town, out in full force.

Jaime, the requesting rider, was one of those 'ghosts'. Perhaps, 'zombie" would be a better characterization. When I arrived at the edge of the pizza shop parking area, I called her to alert her of my arrival. As expected, she indicated she would be "right out", as she had to gather her friends up. The translation of right out usually means in 10 minutes or so. So, I slid into the parking lot space, turned up the radio, and opened up my phone to check my Facebook.

Eventually, a beautiful college-aged blonde walked out of the crowded pizza joint and head towards the car.

"HARVEY. 'SSUP?!!!" she screamed.

I put on the fake-smiley face I make when someone approaches me as if we know each other, just in case I have actually met them before. The fake smile can always be re-configured into a real smile just in case I do in fact know them.

"Hey Jaime! How are you doing tonight?", I said with pseudo-excitement as I examined her face carefully to see if I recognized her. I did not. She was just 'tipsy'. And when you are 'tipsy', everyone is familiar, and everyone is a friend.

"Dude, this is a nice 'whip'!", she howled as she whipped out her cell phone to call the rest of her crew, who were only standing a few feet away in the crowded pizza joint. "Whip" is the newest word for "vehicle". I think it came out of one of recent monthly Chris Brown songs, but I can't say I keep up with the new vernacular.

I thanked her, and went back to scanning my Facebook timeline to pass the time, while we waited for her friends to filter in.

She says " I get it...." noticing the attention I was paying to my Facebook, "You're an '*INTROVERT*', right?. I'm not like that. I am definitely an OUTROVERT!"

I cringed momentarily as I carried the shame that her parents must be feeling with all the money they wasted on her college education, only to have her wreck and ruin a simple antonym.

Eventually, her friends slithered out of the bar, among the fifty or so exiting patrons, who had no reason to stay, now that the basketball game had concluded. One-by-one, she convinced each one to get into my 'whip', so they could continue the party at the next venue, seven miles away at the Sooner Bowling Center. Yes, the bowling alley.

Even the level of inebriation of Jaime's friends didn't make going to the local bowling alley an easy sell. But the promise of more alcohol was the selling point that worked on everyone, except on the last friend, Jenny. Jenny, who was also her roommate, just said, rather unconvincingly after a few minutes of declining the offer, that she would go to the bowling alley. But, she said that she needed to drop by "Charlie's" a nearby "hookah" establishment first. None of us believed her. So, we moved on.

Jaime was not pleased with Jenny. She asked me "I can't stand her sometimes. By the way, have you ever seen a girl with a head that big?"

I knew I should have left that attempt to bring me into a conversation alone. But, I disregarded my common sense and took the bait.

"Sure, her head is probably bigger-than-average, but it's not that bad." I said.

"No, dude, her head is HUUUUUGE. You should see her in a ball cap. She wears a size-8 or -9." Jaime said as the friends in the car laughed.

I have no idea about how to grade hat sizes. I assume that size-8 is large. But if you've lived your whole life in Oklahoma, the cowboy hat capital of the universe, this is a thing you just know. So, I took her word for it.

"Well, I'm not sure. I don't think it's funny. There are medical reasons that a persons head could be that big..."

Although throwing the "medical reasons" card at people who are making fun of someone's deformity usually puts a chill on the laughter, it did not work on this crowd. They laughed even harder, almost surely guaranteeing themselves a front-row seat in hell.

"What medical problem could make your head that big?" she asked, between laughs.

If "outrovert" was part of her vocabulary, I doubt the word "hydrocephalus" would be in there too. So, I chose another angle.

"Put it like this," I said "Having a large head could provide some advantages you normal-sized head people don't have."

"Like what?" she asked

I didn't have a prepared answer for that question, so I winged it.

I said "Well, if she gets bitten by a mosquito carrying the Zika virus while she is pregnant, maybe the size of the baby's head will end up normal."

There was no laughter at that response. They all just shook their heads like they learned something new. WOW. They turned out to be as dumb as I thought they were.

"Do you have an Aux cord?" She then asked as a new idea popped into her head.

"No" I said in a verbal reflex as quick as a ninja. I've learned that this question is a segue into my eardrums exploding as they take my car stereo hostage with bad music at maximal decibels. Despite my response, she discovered that I had Sirius XM, which to a drunk college student is an acceptable next-best-weapon to destroy a driver's hearing.

A few street turns, and she came up with another stop we needed to make along the way to pick up a couple more of her friends who remained in town. It turned out they had all just graduated, and these were to be among their last days. And they were intending to go out with a bang.

We ended up on Elm street and picked an additional two passengers to my delight. Now, the ride would have to be upgraded from basic "X" to "XL"(the fare for more than 4 riders), which would pay double to the fare that I would receive when the ride was over. Almost instantly, my mood changed from "foul" to "fun", as I realized that no matter what happened or how bad my psyche or eardrums got damaged , I would be taken care of financially.

"You're so cool, Harvey" Jaime said as she flipped through the channels of Sirius XM radio. She landed on the 80's Channel. The song "She's Fly" by Tony Terry. I had almost forgotten this song which came out in the late 80's and how good it was. She seemed to sing along as she amped the volume towards its maximum and began bobbing her head and neck as if she had a neurological condition. I was surprised that she seemed to know this song, as it was only a minor hit that came out before she was even born.

"You got any weed?" she said out-of-nowhere. I always hate when someone asks me that question, as it clearly has racial and lifestyle stereotypes and connotations, that I don't feel I fit. I just rolled my eyes and responded "No, but I could ask my parole officer. I'm sure he would know somebody. Oh Wait. Or maybe you could ask a drug dealer or college student." This seemed like a better answer than answering with a demographic reality check like "Why are you asking a middle-aged black guy with nerd glasses this question." Then I thought about it. A Cadillac Escalade does leave the impression that you may know your way around the thug life and drug life. So, maybe her question was a fair one. Immediate laughter filled the car to break the tension, and it spared me from throwing the snarky and offensive verbal boomerangs and javelins that I wanted to throw. With my answer, she whipped out her cell phone to call a few "suppliers" she knew, as I turned a deaf ear to her attempt to score a drug which is still illegal in Oklahoma. Thankfully, she was not successful, and I would downright refuse to make another unplanned stop to allow her to pickup a drug stash.

As we got closer to the bowling alley, one of Jaime's male friends in the back noted that with the 15-minute ride, they would only have about 30 minutes to bowl before the alley shut down at 12. What were they thinking. A regular bar would be open til 2AM. If the goal was to pickle their livers and wake up in the morning hungover with regrets, a regular bar was the way to go. Drunk logic, however, dictated that tonight was a night to bowl. Unfortunately, the night manager of the bowling alley was not on the same page as them. He was a portly guy in his mid-thirties, with a build similar to the Pilsbury doughboy, but with a huge tuft of frontal hair that would have made Vidal Sassoon proud. It was obvious to everyone that his hair did not match his overall look. He was putting his key in the door the minute we drove into its almost barren parking lot.

HEYYY!!! She screamed at the manager." What are you doing?"

"We're closing early. We close early when things are dead" he said.

"But we just got here. We came to PART-AYYY!" she screamed back with a slurring that made her drunken condition obvious. To her credit, they were not due to close for another thirty minutes, according to the hours of operation written on the door he was closing. In spite of the futility of the situation, she opened the car door and ran up towards the bowling-alley entrance to engage the manager.

"Aww, Man, C'mon! Please?! There are 6 of us. We'll make it worth your while." Jaime pleaded to the unsympathetic night manager.

Almost smirking, he ran his finger to his well-conditioned frontal body wave of hair, and said "Sorry. I have already clocked out. The 'computer' wouldn't let me back in, even if I tried."

I smirked as he said it. Every word he said just proved he was not the owner of this business. An owner wouldn't have to clock in. An owner of a business like this on a slow night would have gladly put in another half-hour to score a couple of hundred dollars in beer and bowling.

After a few more minutes of desperate pleading while the more sober comrades watched in annoyance, Jaime resigned herself to the reality that tonight was going to be free of bowling. She yelled in comical exasperation, "What's your name?"

'Derek," he said.

She said Well, DAMN YOU, Derek!"

He looked at her in shock.

'DAMN YOU and DAMN YOUR MAMA!" she continued. Any hope of him changing his mind was probably lost forever at that point.

'DAMN YOUR MAMA'S MAMA!"

<Silence>

And to finish it off, she yelled a final damnation, "DAMN YOUR DAUGHTER'S MAMA!"

A collective groan escaped from the mouths of everybody who witnessed this scene. It may have been fair to damn the man, and maybe his mama too. Even, damning his grandma could have been rationalized as reasonable. But damning his daughter's mama? That was cold. That was gangsta. Had Derek decided to deck her, I doubt if anyone would have tried to stop him.

By that time, Derek had hopped into the driver seat of the only other car in the parking lot, and put the key in the ignition and, visibly laughing, as he drove away. I realized that despite the wasted time, that now I would have to drive them somewhere else. This meant more money for me, which I probably need to buy ear plugs or to get fitted for hearing aids. I was so glad to be on Obamacare at that moment.

As the group collected themselves, and considered their options of where they would spend the last of their drinking hours, I headed back towards our original pick up place, the Pizza Joint in Campus Corner. They decided they would go to "Charlie's", which was just a few yards away. I bid my new variable drunken and weedless friends a good night as they exited the car.

I was thankful that their ride alone, along with fare upgrade due to the number of passengers, had allowed me to exceed my quota for that night. With that knowledge, I turned my apps off, and flipped the radio back to "Smooth Jazz" and relaxed during the long drive home.

<Jimmy Jimmy>

Chapter 9

The Life of Luxury

I remember the first time I picked up Don. I had only been driving for Uber for about a month and was still quite wet behind the ears as far as driving goes. It was at his house, which conveniently was just two neighborhoods over from where I live. He emerged of his darkened house, at 10pm and came over to the car. He was an intimidating figure, in his 50's I thought, tall, rugged looking, big powerful hands and long brown hair fastened into a man bun. He wasn't a hipster, though. He was too old for that. He opened the car door and asked if he could sit up front. I said "Sure". As he got in, his breath reeked of gin or vodka. His menacing stature seemed to dissolve immediately as he began to speak. He was friendly, easy to converse with, and gentle, not at all what I expected. And as I studied his face, I could see he was a probably a few years younger than what I thought he may have been initially. A life of hard work, out in the sun, had prematurely aged him. It was obvious to me although he was clearly lucid, there was no way he should not be driving. As I tapped on the app to enter the pickup and figure out where we were going, I noticed he had not yet entered a destination. So, I asked him.

Where are we headed tonight, Sir?!" I asked.

I was thinking about 'Red Rock Grill' by the lake. You been there?" he responded

"Oh a few times. I really like that place. The view of lake Hefner is hypnotic.... The food is terrific. Nice choice." I said, although I thought it might be a little late to start a Thursday night of fun there.

After minutes of deliberation as we drove several miles towards the Red Rock, he changed his mind, and said. "No, you're right. They may be closing down soon. Let's try 'Little Darlings' instead."

'Little Darlings', the Crown jewel of the seedy Strip Club district known as Valley Brook was miles away in the opposite direction.   But, I didn't really care that he changed his mind.   More miles meant a higher fare. Besides, he seemed to be a nice man. I thought his conversation was entertaining. I could tell he liked me too.

'Little Darlings' is a popular destination for both locals and visitors to our area. Some call it "Little D" for obvious reasons. And others call it "Quadruple D", also for reasons you can probably imagine. Most people, however, who visit are unaware of the notoriety it has of being dangerous. I get really surprised if a month goes by and there is not a shooting or two.   Surprisingly, the street it's on is lined with 3 or 4 other nudie bars or swinger clubs, none of which have the majestic neon Vegas treatment that "Little Darlings" building has with its huge sign, canopied driveway, and lighted exterior. The street, however, offers something for every taste and perversion, specifically anyone suffering from a case of the small town "hornz".

The confusing city ordinances in Valley Brook make it challenging for people who frequent these clubs to remain on the right side of the law. For example, the strip clubs are permitted to serve alcohol on premises. That makes sense, since you can have a lot more fun at a strip club when you are liquored up.   The clubs on the street that offer "full nudity", however, are not permitted to serve or have alcohol on the premises. That makes no sense. People who like partially naked or fully naked women gyrating up and down poles or doing the 'seismic shimmy' on their laps just love alcohol. It's the same damn crowd.   Well, I think the Valley Brook lawmakers tried to pull a fast one by enacting that ordinance, in an effort to put a chill on the full nude business.

It turns out that the joke was on them when the ladies and bouncers tried to undermine the ordinance by offering vodka-infused jelly beans to their patrons.   I'm told that you can perfuse enough alcohol into the jelly beans, such that if you scarf down enough of them, you can rival any cocktail that they could make in a regular bar.   That, my friends, was an "Einstein move", because it took brains, not beauty, to come up with that idea. But it didn't last for long. One of the patrons, who accepted the loaded jelly beans and was offered a "seismic shimmy", turned out to be an undercover police officer from the Valley Brook PD. That club is now shut down. It seems that silicone poisoning from the over-sized breast implants can affect your thinking and judgment. The police department is the next building down from the line of clubs. So someone with the true intellect of Einstein, or way less, could have predicted this outcome.

The owner of "Little Darlings", a woman in her sixties, who has seen many shutdowns in her time, blamed the 'busty Einsteins' for not following the rules. She fired all of the girls, the bouncer, and the DJ, and vowed to begin again and rise from the ashes like a scantily clad phoenix. She had done so a number of times. In the press accounts of the shutdown, she seemed "shocked" that something like this could happen. She obviously believes we were all born yesterday. And I'm sure that 'new beginning' will start with a nice hefty pay-off to one of the elective officials, much to the chagrin of the Police Department.

So we drive up to the canopy under the glare of the beautiful neon sign complete with the image of an beautiful, curvy woman, impossibly proportioned woman with a welcoming face, and I bid Don "adieu" and wished him a good time.

He shook my hand, and asked what he need to do to settle the bill. I knew immediately that this was his first time using Uber. So, I explained, how it works and that everything was taken care of. Even with that, he offered a twenty-dollar tip, that he shucked from a large roll of cash in his pocket and gave to me. I thanked him. And then he asked if I would be available to pick him up in a few hours. Uber only allows the nearest driver to be summoned through the app. But it was clear that he liked me and trusted me, and I knew the route to his home, even if he was too obtunded to know it himself. I gave him my personal number and just told him to call me directly, and I would come and get him. I hadn't planned to be out late that night, but for him, I would make it an exception.

At 1:45AM, as I slept lightly, my cell phone rang. It was Don. He was ready to be picked up. So, I Shrugged off the remnants of slumber, jumped in the car and headed over to "Little Darlings". He was right there waiting under the canopy. He stumbled getting in the car. The smell of alcohol was even stronger than it had been before. But, he was grateful for the ride. As we left the parking lot, and turned onto the street, I could see a car in the distance behind me, flip its headlights on. This was followed by flashing lights on its roof.

"Damn" I thought as the I came to a stop. The officer from the vehicle walked to the driver side of my car, as I had already readied myself to show ID and driver's registration, although I wasn't sure what I did to precipitate this stop. He shined he flashlight into my eyes, which made me squint, and then into my drunken passenger's eyes.

He said "Sir, do you know why I stopped you?"

I said " Honestly, sir, no I do not." I had barely just got out of the parking lot and didn't have time to accelerate to speed above that street's limit.

He then posed a non-sequitir question "How much have you had to drink this evening, sir?"

As a non-drinker, my response to this question is always peppered with schock and indignation.

I said " Sir, nothing. I don't drink alcohol."

He followed up with his last question " Then what are you doing here at this club?"
With this questions, I immediately knew why I was stopped. I was a farming expedition for a DUI ticket. Anyone exiting that club at closing was most likely to be drunk. Realizing this is what he was thinking, I said " Oh, I am an Uber Driver. I am picking up a rider here"

I showed him the open Uber app on my phone and he slapped his head, like he had just missed winning a poker hand, and immediately walked away after saying "OK". Sadly, the scene repeats itself like a broken highlight real every time I pickup someone or drop off someone on this street.

Don made me aware that this is a common occurrence coming back from "Little D", and he couldn't afford to get another DUI. So, when he drinks, he always makes arrangements for a ride. He was far too incoherent for us to have a meaningful conversation about how the night went. So I let him talk until he dozed off during the ride to his house. I woke him up when we arrived. He thanked me, and asked if he could call again the next time he want to go out. I told him "Of course". He pulled out a smaller circular wad of cash, and shucked another twenty-dollar bill off and handed it to me appreciatively. And I drove back to my house and hopped into bed, without disturbing Vargas and Merkel, my chihuahuas.

Over the next several months, Don made good on his offer to call. I got to know him well. He wasn't fifty. He was 43. When he kept referring to me like a little brother, I had to reveal that I was actually older than him. He found that funny. He was a combat veteran who served during the Iraq War. He was a gun collector, but not a "gun nut". He was an experienced aircraft mechanic, but had retired from it after a few injuries. He was actually remodeling the house that I picked him up from. He was gonna sell it when he was done, and find another house to flip and repeat the same process. He made a good living doing that. To have such a "hard" life look to him, he actually was living a good life. He had married and divorced, had an adult son, and love to take long road-trips in his van which he had converted to quite a mobile living space. He even had internet and cable access for his van. Having no attachments to hold him down or schedule to restrict, he was essentially a free spirit. He seemed happy. But, I detected a void. We all have them.

Drinking was a staple in his existence. I tried to ask him about it without seeming like I was judging him. He always smelled like alcohol. And every time I picked him up from the bar, smelled like he had drunken even more. He acknowledged that he liked his alcohol, but he didn't think he was an alcoholic. One night, he called me. It was not for a pick up. He wanted to just go to the convenience store to pick up some stomach medicine. He said he didn't feel well. I headed over to his house. He approached the car slowly. It was clear when I saw him that something was wrong. When he got into the car, I could see the pain in his eyes. We talked about his belly pain. Although I couldn't tell for sure if his eyes were jaundiced, I couldn't leave it on my conscience if something was seriously wrong with him. I made the case to him to go to the local emergency room. He was in so much pain, and had been unable to eat for a couple of days, he did not resist. I dropped him off. My experience with ER doctors led me to prepare him for the possibility of being treated like a drunk. In the back of my mind, I knew that it was possible that he could have a serious medical issue like pancreatitis or a liver problem. I told him to call me when the doctor had evaluated him and to call me to pick him up when they released him.

He called for me to pick him up from the hospital 3 days later. It was pancreatitis. He had come to the realization that drinking was having an impact on his health and the quality of life. He said that he knew he couldn't quit, but he believed he could certainly cut down. That was a good start.

About two weeks later, on a Friday night, he called me to come get him. He had gotten a haircut. The ponytail/man-bun was gone. He looked less hardened, more like the average Joe. He looked good actually. There was color in his skin and his eyes were clear. When he jumped in the car, he was excited to tell me how much he had cut down. I believed him. He didn't even smell like a distillery. Off to "Little D" we went. He told me to look for him around closing time for a ride home. Like clockwork, shortly before 2AM, I got the call to return to pick him up.

But this time, he was clear-minded. He said he had a good time, and even met someone.

"One of the dancers?" I asked.

"Yes," he answered. "She's real pretty. I think she likes me too. I don't know, though. She could be playing me along."

I agreed with him. The women in these places have to be shrewd. In addition to doing their jobs, they have to be careful to avoid men who are forceful or violent. They have to avoid being victimized in so many ways. I wouldn't be surprised if a number of those women dancing at these clubs actually hate men. What they must put up. It's not fun for them. It's a job. It's no surprise that some are strong enough to manipulate the emotions of lonely and drunk men. Thank goodness for closing time, that probably protected Don from getting shaken down for all his money.

"She gave me her number and told me to call her sometime. I think I'm gonna do it." he said.

I was silent.

I dropped him off at home and watched him walk to the front door and enter. I could not help but imagine how lonely he must have been.

Saturday, the next night, he called. As I expected, he wanted to be taken to the Strip club, but 9PM was a bit earlier than the usual outing time for him. I was correct and incorrect at the same time. He wanted to go to "Little D", but only to meet the dancer there and take her out for dinner....a legitimate date. She wasn't working that night. And the Club obviously was a good mutual place to meet.

After entering the club and having me wait, he came back out and got in the car. I felt bad for him. It seemed as if he was stood up. He said to drive him down the road to the convenience store underneath the highway underpass. He said she would meet him there, as she was not allowed to be seen leaving with patrons of the club. This was one of the Club rules.

After a few minutes, a black stretch limo pulled up to the convenience store parking lot. The door opened at out step a foot hooved in an expensive Louboutin pump, followed by a beautiful human form with impossibly small waist and the face of a cover model. Her skin was the beautiful color of espresso or macchiato color. Although I was not expecting his dancer to look as beautiful or to be someone of a different race, I was impressed with his taste and the ability to look past skin color and occupation and allow his attraction to occur naturally without limitation or qualification.

As she entered my vehicle, Don made the introduction.

"This is my driver, Harvey, the one I've been telling you about.", he said to the beauty.

"Hi Harvey. It is so good to meet you. I'm Luxury." she said with a smile.

"Hi Luxury" I said, having to contain myself after hearing her name. I must admit that this name suited her.

Off to Red Rock Grill we went. I pretended to be the professional driver that I felt they expected me to be. So, I shut up, turned up the romantic music and drove. I pretended to ignore the lovey-dovey talk and the kissing in the back seat, like a chauffeur would have done. Like a gentleman, he exited first when we reached the entrance of the Red Rock Grill, and opened her door, and helped her out of the vehicle. He winked and said he would call me later when they needed to be picked up.

When I returned nearly 3 hours later, I could tell they both had a good time, and that they really appreciated each others company. I presumed that we would either be riding back to his house or her place. I waited for directions, until Don told me I'd be dropping him off at home, and then I would drive her to her place. He told me not to worry about the fare. He would take care of it. At his house he gave the beautiful woman a deep kiss, and a promise to call her in the morning. I had never seen him smile so much. This was real.

She asked me if we could stop by the Burger King drive-thru on our way to her place. She was living in a hotel next to the interstate, and there was a BK right next to it. On our way, she opened herself up a bit and just starting talking.   I got to learn her story and her "Truth". Her truth was "Blue", filled with hardship, hard knocks, dark times, bad choices and lessons learned. She wasn't sure if a relationship with him was possible. She had been in a few bad ones. She had two kids, whose fathers were "no good". One had been abusive, putting her at times to within inches of her life. She dreamed of one day, going back to school, and maybe becoming a nurse. Right now, exotic dancing paid the bills. And she wasn't sure how long she could keep doing it. Luxury was raised in the church. She sang in the choir. And she felt the upbringing she had was making her feel terribly conflicted with her choices.   The choice to dance had kept her estranged from her mother and siblings. They, she pointed out, still belong to the church.

 We both agreed that Don was an all-around good guy.   She acknowledged that when he asked her out on the date, she questioned his motives.   She never knew that he had also been apprehensive and questioned hers.   Only, I knew what both of them didn't.   He turned out to be a gentleman, and despite their differences, they were a match of souls.

I was impressed with her. Not only was she beautiful, beneath all the makeup, the hair extensions, the snazzy outfit and the Louboutin knock-offs, but she was intelligent, well-spoken and introspective. She was a great complement to the gruff gentleman she went out on the date with. It was clear that she was still the good girl she was raised to be, but time, choices and circumstances led her to a life she was not comfortable with. She was still someone's mother and someone's child. She still deserved someone's love. She had done a lot of living for someone in her twenties. For what it lacked in triumphs and material luxury, it more than made up for in richness of experience.

At the drive thru speaker, I placed the order for her: Two Whopper Jrs., french fries, a vanilla milkshake and two orders of chicken fries. The cashier broadcasted the total back to me which was around eight dollars.

She said "Thanks, but I didn't order any chicken fries."

I said " Girl, those chicken fries ain't for you. They mine. Just pay the man and mind ya business."

She chuckled, but pulled out ten dollars from her purse and paid the bill. My counseling services, no matter how weak you think they are, are not free.

I asked her during the short ride from the drive-thru to the motel, if she thought she would see Don again. She thought a moment before saying. "Maybe." Something in the way she said "Maybe" made me think that she was just being polite. I guess I would never know. Anyhow, as she got out of the car with her bag of food, I asked her in the most fatherly way possible "Aren't you forgetting something?"

She smiled embarrassingly and said " Oh, yes. What do I owe you?"

I said "Nothing. Don took care of the ride. I was asking about the barbecue sauce that goes with these chicken fries I'm tryna eat."

She laughed again, but fished out the little containers of sauce from her bag. And just like a vision, she vanished into the dark blueness of night.

Several months and a few seasons passed by. I had not heard from Don. I figured that he had probably finished the remodeling project and moved on to the next one. Maybe he quit drinking and swore off of going out. One day out of the blue, he popped into my mind, like in my former profession, when I thought of a patient I hadn't seen in a while. It happened like a sixth-sense. With my patients, it usually meant they had moved somewhere. And sometimes, it meant that they had found a new doctor. Sometimes, I would learn why I had not seen them by scanning the weekly obituary in the newspaper. Don was not my patient. He was just a rider, but one that I cared about.

I searched for his cell number in my phone, figuring I would call him just to say hello and to make sure he was doing okay. To my surprise, a woman answered the phone. When I asked if Don was there, she replied that he wasn't, and asked who was calling. I identified myself as Harvey, and old friend, who just called to see how he was doing. When I asked what time he'd be back in, she revealed that Don had died, two months ago.

My first instinct was to ask questions, like "Why?," "How?" or "What happened?". But as soon as I thought of asking those questions, I realized how inappropriate that asking them may have been. And I relented to the shock and dismay of being caught off-guard and I began the process of grieving the loss my late friend. I told the woman who had answered the phone that I was sorry. The conversation ended in silence.

Within a couple of days, I began thinking about Don again. Wondering if over the time I knew him, he had gotten what he deserved from his short life. He was a war vet, and traveled extensively. He had a kid he watched grow up. He drank heavily, either to drown his sorrows that he could not articulate in any other way except through the escape that alcohol provides. I wondered if he actually got close to finding the love he was looking for and filling that void.

One day recently, I found myself making a turn on the road towards his neighborhood. I turned on his street, just hoping I could see him walk out of his house, one more time. As I approached his house, I got the answer to the most lingering question I had about Don. A beautiful woman was sitting on the porch with a a self-assured smile, enjoying the summer breeze. It was Luxury. She was his True Blue love. I smiled. And drove away quickly before she had a chance to recognize me or the car.   My question as to whether he found love in his life was answered in full.

I believe in fairytales again.

<True Blue>

Check Out My Other Books...

Below are some of my other great titles, which if you liked this book, I am confident you will enjoy as well.

The Patient's Guide to Pain Management: What You Need to Know to Navigate Through the Stigma to Get the Care that You Need

This book teaches you in simple, understandable language how to navigate through the stigma that encompasses people in pain to find the care that you need. It explains how to find a doctor, what to expect when you are there, and how to avoid the "traps" of being "fired" as a patient. As the climate of treating pain and seeking pain treatment become increasing repressive, this guide will put you ahead of game, so you can worry about the more important things in life, and not just your pain.

Available on:

Amazon Kindle: *http://amzn.to/1GyCpfH*

5 Ways to Effortlessly Outsmart your Pain Doctor: What You Need to Know to Navigate Through the Battlefield of Pain Management to Get the Care that You Need

Pain Management is a war, a war that is being waged on you. If you are not careful, one of your potential enemies in this war will be your own doctor. This book teaches you about the tactics and the traps that are being used in this war. You will learn specific ways to mount your counter-offensive, so that you can win each battle and the war. And most importantly, using these strategies, you will be able to get the care you need.

Available on:

Amazon Kindle: *http://amzn.to/1b3sBhb*

Private Driver: Confessions of a Ride-Share Cabbie

The story of how I went from Harvard-Trained Spine surgeon to Ride-share driver is a story for another day and another book. And, trust me, that book, although as yet unwritten, is coming. It will be the most compelling story that I have to tell.   Suffice it to say, this abrupt professional transition in my life has provided me with a new set of lenses to view the world__ a part of the world I missed when I was submerged in my training to become a physician. Now I have new "vision", and I like what I am seeing. It is in that spirit, I share some of my funniest experiences from what I call the UberSphere- 'Lyftmosphere'- 'Side-Carnival' or the World of Ride-sharing Services.

Available on:

Amazon Kindle: *http://amzn.to/1NCPoP4*

Private Driver: Pull Up to the Bumper, Confessions, Part 2

The story continues in this sequel that will have you rolling on the floor with laughter. I share more of my funniest experiences from what I cal the UberSphere- 'Lyftmosphere'- 'Side-Carnival' or the World of Ride-sharing Services.

Available on:

Amazon Kindle: *http://amzn.to/1h6NWdw*

Private Driver: Smooth Uber Rider, Confessions, Part 3

More stories from the world of ride-sharing with some of the funniest people in Oklahoma.

Available on:

Amazon Kindle: *http://amzn.to/1hsGWHe*

Private Driver: Blood on The Dashboard, Confessions, Part 4

Just when you thought it was over. Even more stories from the world of ride-sharing with some of the funniest people in Oklahoma.

Available on:

Amazon Kindle: *http://amzn.to/1WM3Yfb*

Grab your copy today and dive into the fascinating world of Pain Management and Ride-Share.

If for some reason these links do not seem to be working, you can search for any of these titles directly on Amazon to grab them.

One Last Thing…

When you turn the page, Kindle will give you the opportunity to rate the book and share your thoughts on Facebook and Twitter. If you believe the book is worth sharing, would you take a few seconds to let your friends know about it? If it turns out to make a difference in their lives, they'll be forever grateful to you. As will I.

All the best,
Harvey Jenkins MD PhD

Printed in Great Britain
by Amazon